Adele: A Biography

Adele is an English singer-songwriter. Gradu

Performing Arts and Technology in 2006, Adele was given a recording

contract by XL Recordings after a friend posted her demo on Myspace the

same year. In 2007, she received the Brit Awards "Critics' Choice" award

and won the BBC Sound of 2008 poll. Her debut album, 19, was released in

2008 to commercial and critical success. It is certified seven times platinum

in the UK, and three times platinum in the US. An appearance she made on

Saturday Night Live in late 2008 boosted her career in the US. At the 51st

Grammy Awards in 2009, Adele received the awards for Best New Artist

and Best Female Pop Vocal Performance.

Adele released her second studio album, 21, in early 2011. The album was

well received critically and surpassed the success of her debut, earning the

singer numerous awards in 2012, among them a record-tying six Grammy

Awards, including Album of the Year; two Brit Awards, including British

Album of the Year, and three American Music Awards. The album has been

certified 16 times platinum in the UK, and is the fourth best-selling album in

the UK of all time. In the US it has held the top position longer than any album since 1985, and is certified Diamond. The album has sold 31 million copies worldwide.

The success of 21 earned Adele numerous mentions in the Guinness Book of World Records. She is the first woman in the history of the Billboard Hot 100 to have three simultaneous top 10 singles as a lead artist, and the first female artist to simultaneously have two albums in the top five of the Billboard 200 and two singles in the top five of the Billboard Hot 100. 21 is the longest-running number one album by a female solo artist in the history of the UK and US Album Charts. In 2012, she released "Skyfall", which she wrote and recorded for the James Bond film of the same name. The song won an Academy Award, a Grammy Award, and a Golden Globe Award for Best Original Song. After taking a three-year break, Adele released her third studio album, 25, in 2015. It became the year's best-selling album and broke first week sales records in the UK and US. 25 was her second album to be certified Diamond in the US. The lead single, "Hello", became the first song in the US to sell over one million digital copies within a week of its release. Her third concert tour, Adele Live 2016, is her largest to date, taking in Europe, North America and Oceania, and will end with four concerts at Wembley Stadium, London in mid 2017.

In 2011, 2012 and 2016, Billboard named Adele Artist of the Year. In 2012, she was listed at number five on VH1's 100 Greatest Women in Music. Time magazine named her one of the most influential people in the world in 2012 and 2016. With sales of more than 100 million records, Adele is one of the best-selling recording artists in the world.

Early life

Adele Laurie Blue Adkins was born on 5 May 1988 in Tottenham, London, the daughter of an English mother, Penny Adkins, and a Welsh father, Marc Evans. Evans left when Adele was two, leaving her mother to raise her. She began singing at age four and asserts that she became obsessed with voices. Growing up, Adele spent most of her time singing rather than reading; the last book she read was Roald Dahl's Matilda when she was six years old. In 1997, at the age of nine, Adele and her mother, who by then had found work as a furniture maker and an adult-learning activities organiser, relocated to Brighton on the south coast of England.

In 1999, two years later, she and her mother moved back to London; first to Brixton, and then to neighbouring district West Norwood, in south London. West Norwood is the subject for Adele's first record, "Hometown Glory", which she wrote and composed in 2004, when she was 16. Adele graduated from the BRIT School for Performing Arts & Technology in Croydon in May 2006, where she was a classmate of Leona Lewis and Jessie J. Adele credits the school with nurturing her talent even though, at the time, she was more interested in going into A&R and hoped to launch other people's careers.

Career

Four months after graduation, she published two songs on the fourth issue of the online arts publication PlatformsMagazine.com. She had recorded a three-song demo for a class project and given it to a friend. The friend posted the demo on Myspace, where it became very successful and led to a phone call from Richard Russell, boss of the music label XL Recordings. She doubted if the offer was real because the only record company she knew was Virgin Records, and she took a friend with her to the meeting.

Nick Huggett, at XL, recommended Adele to manager Jonathan Dickins at September Management, and in June 2006, Dickins became her official representative. September was managing Jamie T at the time and this proved a major draw for Adele, a big fan of the British singer-songwriter. Huggett then signed Adele to XL in September 2006. Adele provided vocals for Jack Peñate's song, "My Yvonne," for his debut album, and it was during this session she first met producer Jim Abbiss, who would go on to produce both the majority of her debut album, 19, and tracks on 21. In June 2007, Adele made her television debut, performing "Daydreamer" on the BBC's Later... with Jools Holland. Adele's breakthrough song, "Hometown Glory", was released in October 2007.

By 2008, Adele had become the headliner and performed an acoustic set, in which she was supported by Damien Rice. She became the first recipient of the Brit Awards Critics' Choice and was named the number-one predicted breakthrough act of 2008 in an annual BBC poll of music critics, Sound of 2008. The album 19, named for her age at the time she wrote and composed many of its songs, entered the British charts at number one. The Times Encyclopedia of Modern Music named 19 an "essential" blue-eyed soul recording. She released her second single, "Chasing Pavements", on 14 January 2008, two weeks ahead of her debut album, 19. The song reached number two on the UK Chart, and stayed there for four weeks. Adele was nominated for a 2008 Mercury Prize award for 19. She also won an Urban Music Award for "Best Jazz Act." She also received a Q Awards nomination in the category of Breakthrough Act and a Music of Black Origin nomination in the category of Best UK Female. In March 2008, Adele signed a deal with Columbia Records and XL Recordings for her foray into the United States. She embarked on a short North American tour in the same month, and 19 was released in the US in June. Billboard magazine stated of it: "Adele truly has potential to become among the most respected and inspiring international artists of her generation." The An Evening with Adele world tour began in May 2008 and ended in June 2009.

She later cancelled the 2008 US tour dates to be with a former boyfriend. She said in Nylon magazine in June 2009, "I'm like, 'I can't believe I did that.' It seems so ungrateful.... I was drinking far too much and that was kind of the basis of my relationship with this boy. I couldn't bear to be without him, so I was like, 'Well, I'll just cancel my stuff then.'" She referred to this period as her "early life crisis". She is also known for her dislike of flying and bouts of homesickness when away from her native London. By the middle of October 2008, Adele's attempt to break in America appeared to have failed. But then she was booked as the musical guest on 18 October 2008 episode of NBC's Saturday Night Live. The episode, which included an expected appearance by then US vice-presidential candidate Sarah Palin, earned the program its best ratings in 14 years with 17 million viewers. Adele performed "Chasing Pavements" and "Cold Shoulder," and the following day, 19 topped the iTunes charts and ranked at number five at Amazon.com while "Chasing Pavements" rose into the top 25. The album reached number 11 on the Billboard 200 as a result, a jump of 35 places over the previous week. In November 2008 Adele moved to Notting Hill, London after leaving her mother's house, a move that prompted her to give up drinking. The album was certified as gold in February 2009 by the RIAA. By July 2009, the album had sold 2.2 million copies worldwide.

At the 51st Annual Grammy Awards in February 2009, Adele received the award for Best New Artist, in addition to the award for Best Female Pop Vocal Performance for "Chasing Pavements", which was also nominated for Record of the Year and Song of the Year. Adele performed "Chasing Pavements" at the ceremony in a duet with Jennifer Nettles. In 2010, Adele received a Grammy nomination for Best Female Pop Vocal Performance for "Hometown Glory." In April her song "My Same" entered the German Singles Chart after it had been performed by Lena Meyer-Landrut in the talent show contest Unser Star für Oslo, or Our Star for Oslo, in which the German entry to the Eurovision Song Contest 2010 was determined. In late September, after being featured on The X Factor, Adele's version of Bob Dylan's "Make You Feel My Love" re-entered the UK singles chart at number 4. During the 2010 CMT Artists of the Year special, Adele performed a widely publicised duet of Lady Antebellum's "Need You Now" with Darius Rucker. This performance was later nominated for a CMT Music Award.

Adele released her second studio album, 21, on 24 January 2011 in the UK and 22 February in the US. She said that the album was inspired by the break-up with her former partner. The album's sound is described as classic and contemporary country and roots music. The change in sound from her first album was the result of her bus driver playing contemporary music from Nashville when she was touring the American South, and the title reflected the growth she had experienced in the prior two years. Adele told Spin Magazine: "It was really exciting for me because I never grew up around ." 21 hit number 1 in more than 26 countries, including the UK and the US.

An emotional performance of "Someone Like You" at the 2011 Brit Awards on 15 February propelled the song to number one in the UK. Her first album, 19, re-entered the UK album chart alongside 21, while first and second singles "Rolling in the Deep" and "Someone Like You" were in the top 5 of the UK singles chart, making Adele the first living artist to achieve the feat of two top-five hits in both the Official Singles Chart and the Official Albums Chart simultaneously since The Beatles in 1964. Both songs topped the charts in multiple markets and broke numerous sales performance records. Following her performance of "Someone Like You" at the 2011 MTV Video Music Awards, it became Adele's second number-one single on the Billboard Hot 100. By December 2011, 21 sold over 3.4 million copies in the UK, and became the biggest-selling album of the 21st century, overtaking Amy Winehouse's Back to Black, with Adele becoming the first artist ever to sell three million albums in the UK in one calendar year. "Set Fire to the Rain" became Adele's third number one single on the Billboard Hot 100, as Adele became the first artist ever to have an album, 21, hold the number-one position on the Billboard 200 concurrently with three number one singles.

To promote the album, Adele embarked upon the "Adele Live" tour, which sold out its North American leg. In October 2011, Adele was forced to cancel two tours because of a vocal-cord haemorrhage. She released a statement saying she needed an extended period of rest to avoid permanent damage to her voice. In the first week of November 2011 Steven M. Zeitels, director of the Center for Laryngeal Surgery and Voice Rehabilitation at the Massachusetts General Hospital in Boston, performed laser microsurgery on Adele's vocal cords to remove a benign polyp. A recording of her tour, Live at the Royal Albert Hall, was released in November 2011, debuting at number one in the US with 96,000 copies sold, the highest one-week tally for a music DVD in four years, becoming the best-selling music DVD of 2011. Adele is the first artist in Nielsen SoundScan history to have the year's number-one album , number-one single , and number-one music video. At the 2011 American Music Awards on 20 November, Adele won three awards; Favorite Pop/Rock Female Artist, Favorite Adult Contemporary Artist, and Favorite Pop/Rock Album for 21. On 9 December, Billboard named Adele Artist of the Year, Billboard 200 Album of the Year , and the Billboard Hot 100 Song of the Year , becoming the first woman ever to top all three categories.

Following the throat microsurgery, she made her live comeback at the 2012 Grammy Awards in February. She won in all six categories for which she was nominated, making her the second female artist in Grammy history, after Beyoncé, to win that many categories in a single night. Following that success, 21 achieved the biggest weekly sales increase following a Grammy win since Nielsen SoundScan began tracking data in 1991. Adele received the Brit Award for Best British Female Solo Artist, and British Album of the Year presented to her by George Michael. Following the Brit Awards, 21 reached number one for the 21st non-consecutive week in the UK. The album has sold over 4.5 million copies in the UK where it is the fourth best-selling album of all time. In October, the album's sales surpassed 4.5 million in the UK, and in November 10 million in the US. As of 2014, the album has sold 30 million copies worldwide. She has sold an estimated 40 million albums and 50 million singles worldwide. Adele is the only artist or band in the last decade in the US to earn an RIAA Diamond certification for a one disc album in less than two years.

In October 2012, Adele confirmed that she had been writing, composing and recording the theme song for Skyfall, the twenty-third James Bond film. The song "Skyfall," written and composed in collaboration with producer Paul Epworth, was recorded at Abbey Road Studios, and features orchestrations by J. A. C. Redford. Adele stated recording "Skyfall" was "one of the proudest moments of my life." On 14 October, "Skyfall" rose to number 2 on the UK Singles Chart with sales of 92,000 copies bringing its overall sales to 176,000, and "Skyfall" entered the Billboard Hot 100 at number 8, selling 261,000 copies in the US in its first three days. This tied "Skyfall" with Duran Duran's "A View to a Kill" as the highest-charting James Bond theme song on the UK Singles Chart; a record surpassed in 2015 by Sam Smith's "Writing's on the Wall".

"Skyfall" has sold more than two million copies worldwide and earned Adele the Golden Globe Award for Best Original Song and the Academy Award for Best Original Song. In December 2012, Adele was named Billboard Artist of the Year, and 21 was named Album of the Year, making her the first artist to receive both accolades two years in a row. Adele was also named top female artist. The Associated Press named Adele Entertainer of the Year for 2012. The 2013 Grammy Awards saw Adele's live version of "Set Fire to the Rain" win the Grammy Award for Best Pop Solo Performance, bringing her total wins to nine.

On 3 April 2012, Adele confirmed that her third album would likely be at least two years away, stating, "I have to take time and live a little bit. There were a good two years between my first and second albums, so it'll be the same this time." She stated that she would continue writing and composing her own material. At the 2013 Grammy Awards, she confirmed that she was in the very early stages of her third album. She also stated that she will most likely work with Paul Epworth again.

In September 2013, Wiz Khalifa confirmed that he and Adele had collaborated on a song for his upcoming fifth studio album, Blacc Hollywood, though the collaboration did not make the final track listing. In

January 2014, Adele received her tenth Grammy Award with "Skyfall" winning Best Song Written for Visual Media at the 56th Annual Grammy Awards. On the eve of her 26th birthday in May 2014, Adele posted a cryptic message via her Twitter account which prompted media discussion about her next album. The message, "Bye bye 25... See you again later in the year," was interpreted by some in the media, including the Daily Mail and Capital FM, as meaning that her next album would be titled 25 and released later in the year. In 2014, Adele was nominated for nine World Music Awards. In early August, Paul Moss suggested that an album would be released in 2014 or 2015. However, in the October 2014 accounts filed with Companies House by XL Recordings, they ruled out a 2014 release.

On 27 August 2015, Billboard reported that Adele's label, XL Recordings, had intentions of releasing her third studio album sometime in November 2015. Danger Mouse has contributed a song, while Tobias Jesso Jr. has written a track, and Ryan Tedder is "back in the mix after producing and co-writing "Rumour Has It" on 21." At the 72nd Venice International Film Festival in early September 2015, Sia announced that her new single "Alive" was co-written by Adele, and had originally been intended for Adele's third album. On 18 October, a 30-second clip of new material from Adele was shown on UK television during a commercial break on The X Factor. The commercial teases a snippet from a new song from her third album, with viewers hearing a voice singing accompanied by lyrics on a black screen.

In a statement released three days later she confirmed that the album is titled 25, with Adele stating, "My last record was a break-up record, and if I had to label this one, I would call it a make-up record. Making up for lost time. Making up for everything I ever did and never did. 25 is about getting to know who I've become without realising. And I'm sorry it took so long but, you know, life happened." Adele also believes 25 will be her last album with her age as its title, believing that 25 would be the end to a trilogy. On 22 October, Adele confirmed that 25 would be released on 20 November, while the lead single from the album, "Hello" would be released on 23 October. The song was first played on Nick Grimshaw's Radio 1 Breakfast Show on the BBC on the morning of 23 October with Adele interviewed live. The video of "Hello", released on 22 October, was viewed over 27.7 million times on YouTube in its first 24 hours, breaking the Vevo record for the most views in a day, surpassing the 20.1 million views for "Bad Blood" by Taylor Swift. On 28 October, news outlets, including BBC News, reported that "Hello" was being viewed on YouTube an average one million times an hour. "Hello" went on to become the fastest video to hit one billion views on YouTube, which it achieved after 88 days. The song debuted at number one in the UK Singles Chart on 30 October, with first week sales of 330,000 copies, making it the biggest-selling number one single in three years. "Hello" also debuted at number one in many countries around the world, including Australia, France, Canada, New Zealand, Ireland and Germany, and on 2 November, the song debuted at number one on the Billboard Hot 100, becoming the first song in the US to sell at least one million downloads in a week, setting the record at 1.11 million. By the end of 2015, it had sold 12.3 million units globally and was the year's 7th best-selling single.

On 27 October, BBC One announced plans for Adele at the BBC, a one-hour special presented by Graham Norton, in which Adele talks about her new album and performs new songs. This was her first television appearance since performing at the 2013 Academy Awards ceremony, and the show was recorded before a live audience on 2 November for broadcast on 20 November, coinciding with the release of 25. On 27 October it was also announced that the singer would make an appearance on the US entertainment series Saturday Night Live on 21 November. On 30 October, Adele confirmed that she would be performing a one-night-only concert titled Adele Live in New York City at the Radio City Music Hall on 17 November. Subsequently, NBC aired the concert special on 14 December.

On 27 November, 25 debuted at number one on the UK Albums Chart and became the fastest selling album in UK chart history with over 800,000 copies sold in its first week. The album debuted at number one in the US where it sold a record-breaking 3.38 million copies in its first week, the largest single sales week for an album since Nielsen began monitoring sales in 1991. 25 also broke first week sales records in Canada and New Zealand. 25 became the best-selling album of 2015 in a number of countries, including Australia, the UK and the US, where it spent seven consecutive weeks at number one in each country, before being displaced by David Bowie's Blackstar. It was the year's best-selling album worldwide with 17.4 million copies sold in 2015 alone, and has since sold 20 million copies globally. Adele's seven weeks at the top of the UK Albums Chart took her total to 31 weeks at number one in the UK with her three albums, surpassing Madonna's previous record of most weeks at number one for a female act ever in the UK.

In November 2015, Adele's 2016 tour was announced, her first tour since 2011. Beginning in Europe, Adele Live 2016 included four dates at the Manchester Arena in March 2016, eight dates at the O2 Arena, London, with further dates in Ireland, Spain, Germany, Italy and the Netherlands among others. Her North American Tour began in July, with the opening concert in St. Paul, Minnesota on 5 July.

At the 2016 Brit Awards in London on 24 February, Adele received the awards for British Female Solo Artist, British Album of the Year for 25, British Single of the Year for "Hello", and British Global Success, bringing her Brit Award wins to eight. She closed the ceremony by performing "When We Were Young", the second single from 25. While on stage at London's O2 Arena on 17 March, Adele announced that she would be headlining on the Pyramid Stage at the 2016 Glastonbury Festival, which was later confirmed by the festival's organizers. She appeared for a 90-minute fifteen song set at the festival on 25 June, and described the experience as "by far, the best moment of my life so far". As part of her world tour, in February and March 2017, Adele will perform in Australia for the first time, playing outdoor stadiums around the country.

Adele will complete her world tour with four concerts, dubbed "The Finale", at Wembley Stadium, London on 28, 29 June and 1, 2 July 2017. She announced the shows at "the home of football" by singing the England football team's "Three Lions" anthem and also the theme song to the BBC's weekly Premier League football show Match of the Day. She added the 28

June and 2 July dates after the first two dates sold out. At the end of 2016, Billbard named Adele Artist of the Year for the third time, with the Top Billboard 200 album. With 135 million views, Adele's Carpool Karaoke through the streets of London with James Corden, a sketch which featured on Corden's talk show The Late Late Show with James Corden in January 2016, is the biggest YouTube viral video of 2016.

Artistry

Adele has cited the Spice Girls as a major influence in regard to her love and passion for music, stating that "they made me what I am today". Adele impersonated the Spice Girls at dinner parties as a young girl. She stated she was left "heartbroken" when her favourite Spice Girl, Geri Halliwell aka "Ginger Spice", left the group. She has also stated that growing up, she listened to Sinéad O'Connor, The Cure, Dusty Springfield, Celine Dion, and Annie Lennox. One of Adele's earliest influences was Gabrielle, who Adele has admired since the age of five. During Adele's school years, her mother made her an eye patch with sequins which she used to perform as the Hackney born star in a school talent contest. After moving to south London, she became interested in R&B artists such as Aaliyah, Destiny's Child, and Mary J. Blige. Adele says that one of the most defining moments in her life was when she watched Pink perform at Brixton Academy in London. She states: "It was the Missundaztood record, so I was about 13 or 14. I had never heard, being in the room, someone sing like that live I remember sort of feeling like I was in a wind tunnel, her voice just hitting me. It was incredible."

In 2002, aged 14, Adele discovered Etta James and Ella Fitzgerald as she stumbled on the artists' CDs in the jazz section of her local music store. She was struck by their appearance on the album covers. Adele states she then "started listening to Etta James every night for an hour," and in the process was getting "to know my own voice." Adele credits Amy Winehouse and her 2003 album Frank for inspiring her to take up the guitar, stating, "If it wasn't for Amy and Frank, one hundred per cent I wouldn't have picked up a guitar, I wouldn't have written "Daydreamer" or "Hometown " and I wrote "Someone Like You" on the guitar too." She also states that her mother, who is very close to her, exposed her to the music of Aaliyah, Lauryn Hill, Mary J. Blige, and Alicia Keys, all of whom inspired her as well. She is also a fan of Lana Del Rey, Grimes, Chvrches, FKA Twigs, Alabama Shakes, Kanye West, Rihanna, Frank Ocean, Stevie Nicks, and Beyoncé. Adele cited Madonna's album Ray of Light as a "chief inspiration" behind her album 25.

Adele's first album, 19, is of the soul genre, with lyrics describing heartbreak and relationship. Her success occurred simultaneously with several other British female soul singers, with the British press dubbing her a new Amy Winehouse. This was described as a third British Musical Invasion of the US. However, Adele called the comparisons between her and other female soul singers lazy, noting "we're a gender, not a genre". AllMusic wrote that "Adele is simply too magical to compare her to anyone." Her second album, 21, shares the folk and soul influences of her debut album, but was further inspired by the American country and Southern blues music to which she had been exposed during her 2008–09 North American tour An Evening with Adele. Composed in the aftermath of the singer's separation from her partner, the album typifies the near dormant tradition of the confessional singer-songwriter in its exploration of heartbreak, self-examination, and forgiveness. Having referred to 21 as a "break-up record", Adele labelled her third studio album, 25, a "make-up record", adding it was about "Making up for lost time. Making up for everything I ever did and never did." Her yearning for her old self, her nostalgia, and melancholy about the passage of time, is a feature of 25, with Adele stating, "I've had a lot of regrets since I turned 25. And sadness hits me in different ways than it used to. There's a lot of things I don't think I'll ever get 'round to doing."

Adele possesses a contralto vocal range. Rolling Stone reported that following throat surgery her voice had become "palpably bigger and purer-toned", and that she had added a further four notes to the top of her range. Initially, critics suggested that her vocals were more developed and intriguing than her songwriting, a sentiment with which Adele agreed. She has stated: "I taught myself how to sing by listening to Ella Fitzgerald for acrobatics and scales, Etta James for passion and Roberta Flack for control." Her voice has received acclaim from critics. In a review of 19, The Observer said, "The way she stretched the vowels, her wonderful soulful phrasing, the sheer unadulterated pleasure of her voice, stood out all the more; little doubt that she's a rare singer". BBC Music wrote, "Her melodies exude warmth, her singing is occasionally stunning and, ...she has tracks that make Lily Allen and Kate Nash sound every bit as ordinary as they are." For their reviews of 21, The New York Times' chief music critic Jon Pareles commended the singer's emotive timbre, comparing her to Dusty Springfield, Petula Clark, and Annie Lennox: " can seethe, sob, rasp, swoop, lilt and belt, in ways that draw more attention to the song than to the singer". Ryan Reed of Paste magazine regarded her voice as "a raspy, aged-beyond-its-years thing of full-blooded beauty", while MSN Music's Tom Townshend declared her "the finest singer of generation".

Personal life and other ventures

It was reported in January 2012 that Adele had been dating charity entrepreneur and Old Etonian Simon Konecki since the summer of 2011. In June 2012, Adele announced that she and Konecki were expecting a baby. Their son was born on 19 October 2012. On the topic of becoming a parent, Adele has since observed that she "felt like was truly living. I had a purpose, where before I didn't". Adele and Konecki brought a privacy case against a UK-based photo agency that published paparazzi images of their son taken during family outings in 2013. Lawyers working on their behalf accepted damages from the company in July 2014.

Born in Tottenham, north London, and raised in West Norwood, south London, Adele has a working-class London accent that Rolling Stone magazine says has only softened slightly over the years. Politically she is a supporter of the Labour Party, stating in 2011 that she was a "Labour girl through and through." In May 2011, she advocated a lower tax rate for high-income earners; a view counter to that of the Labour Party. In 2015, Adele stated "I'm a feminist, I believe that everyone should be treated the same, including race and sexuality".

She is regarded as an icon for the LGBT community. On 12 June 2016 an emotional Adele dedicated her show in Antwerp, Belgium to the victims of the mass shooting at a gay nightclub in Orlando, Florida earlier that day, adding "The LGBTQ community, they're like my soul mates since I was really young, so I'm very moved by it."

Charity

Adele has performed in numerous charity concerts throughout her career. In 2007 and 2008 she performed at the Little Noise Sessions held at London's Union Chapel, with proceeds from the concerts donated to Mencap which works with people with learning disabilities. In July and November 2008, Adele performed at the Keep a Child Alive Black Ball in London and New York City respectively. On 17 September 2009 she performed at the Brooklyn Academy of Music, for the VH1 Divas event, a concert to raise money for the Save The Music Foundation charity. On 6 December, Adele opened with a 40-minute set at John Mayer's 2nd Annual Holiday Charity Revue held at the Nokia Theatre in Los Angeles. In 2011, Adele gave a free concert for Pride London, a registered charity which arranges LGBT events in London.

Adele has been a major contributor to MusiCares, a charity organisation founded by the National Academy of Recording Arts and Sciences for musicians in need. In February 2009, Adele performed at the 2009 MusiCares charity concert in Los Angeles. In 2011 and 2012, Adele donated autographed items for auctions to support MusiCares. When on tour, Adele requires all backstage visitors to donate a minimum charitable contribution of $US20 for the UK charity SANDS, an organisation dedicated to "supporting anyone affected by the death of a baby and promoting research to reduce the loss of babies' lives". During the UK and European leg of her Adele Live tour, she collected $US13,000 for the charity.

Awards and achievements

At the 51st Annual Grammy Awards in 2009, Adele won awards in the categories of Best New Artist and Best Female Pop Vocal Performance. She was also nominated in the categories of Record of the Year and Song of the Year. That same year, Adele was also nominated for three Brit Awards in the categories of Best British Female, Best British Single and Best British Breakthrough Act. Then British Prime Minister Gordon Brown sent a thank-you letter to Adele that stated "with the troubles that the country's in financially, you're a light at the end of the tunnel."

With 21 non-consecutive weeks at number 1 in the US, Adele broke the record for the longest number-1 album by a woman in Billboard history, beating the record formerly held by Whitney Houston's soundtrack The Bodyguard. 21 spent its 23rd week at number one in March 2012, making it the longest-running album at number one since 1985, and it became the fourth best-selling album of the past 10 years in the US. The best selling album in the UK of the 21st century, 21 is also the fourth best-selling album in the UK of all time, while 25 is currently ranked twenty-sixth all time. Both 21 and 25 have been certified Diamond by the Recording Industry Association of America .

In February 2012, Adele was listed at number five on VH1's 100 Greatest Women in Music. In April 2012, American magazine Time named Adele one of the 100 most influential people in the world. People named her one of 2012 Most Beautiful at Every Age. On 30 April 2012, a tribute to Adele was held at New York City's Poisson Rouge called Broadway Sings Adele, starring various Broadway actors such as Matt Doyle. In July 2012, Adele was listed at number six in Forbes list of the world's highest-paid celebrities under the age of 30, having earned £23 million between May 2011 and May 2012.

On the week ending 3 March 2012, Adele became the first solo female artist to have three singles in the top 10 of the Billboard Hot 100 at the same time, and the first female artist to have two albums in the top 5 of the Billboard 200 and two singles in the top 5 of the Billboard Hot 100 simultaneously. Adele topped the 2012 Sunday Times Rich List of musicians in the UK under 30 and made the Top 10 of Billboard magazine's "Top 40 Money Makers". Billboard also announced the same day that Adele's "Rolling in the Deep" is the biggest crossover hit of the past 25 years, topping pop, adult pop and adult contemporary charts and that Adele is one of four female artists to have an album chart at number one for more than 13 weeks . On 6 March, 21 reached 30 non-consecutive weeks at number one on the Australian ARIA Chart, making it the longest-running number one album in Australia in the 21st century, and the second longest-running number one ever.

At the 2012 Ivor Novello Awards in May, Adele was named Songwriter of the Year, and "Rolling in the Deep" won the award for Most Performed Work of 2011. At the 2012 BMI Awards held in London in October, Adele won Song of the Year in recognition of the song being the most played on US television and radio in 2011.

In 2013, Adele won the Academy Award for Best Original Song for the James Bond theme "Skyfall". This is the first James Bond song to win and only the fifth to be nominated , "Nobody Does It Better" , "Live and Let Die" , and "The Look of Love"). "Skyfall" won the Brit Award for Best British Single at the 2013 Brit Awards.

In June 2013, Adele was appointed a MBE in the Queen's Birthday Honours list for services to music, and she received the award from Prince Charles at Buckingham Palace on 19 December 2013. In February 2013, she was assessed as one of the 100 most powerful women in the United Kingdom by Woman's Hour on BBC Radio 4. In April 2016, Adele appeared for the second time on the Time 100 list of most influential people.

In 2014, Adele was already being regarded as a British cultural icon, with young adults from abroad naming her among a group of people that they most associated with UK culture, which included William Shakespeare, Queen Elizabeth II, David Beckham, J. K. Rowling, The Beatles, Charlie Chaplin and Elton John.

Concert tours

21 is the second studio album by British singer Adele. It was released on 24 January 2011 in most of Europe, and on 22 February 2011 in North America. The album was named after the age of the singer during its production. 21 shares the folk and Motown soul influences of her 2008 debut album 19, but was further inspired by the American country and Southern blues music to which she had been exposed during her 2008–09 North American tour An Evening with Adele. Composed in the aftermath of the singer's separation from her partner, the album typifies the near dormant tradition of the confessional singer-songwriter in its exploration of heartbreak, self-examination, and forgiveness.

Adele began writing 21 in April 2009, when still involved in the relationship that subsequently inspired the record. Dissatisfied with once again portraying herself as the musical tragedian of her debut, she had intended to compose a more upbeat and contemporary follow-up. However, studio sessions ended prematurely due to a lack of inspiration. She resumed production immediately after the breakdown of her relationship, channelling her heartbreak and depression into her songs. Adele collaborated with various songwriters and producers, including Columbia Records co-president Rick Rubin, Paul Epworth, Ryan Tedder, Jim Abbiss, and Dan Wilson.

Praised by critics for its understated production, vintage aesthetic, and Adele's vocal performance, 21 defied the modest commercial expectations of her indie record label XL Recordings. The album topped the charts in more than 30 countries and became the world's best-selling album of the year for 2011 and 2012. In the United Kingdom, it is the best-selling album of the 21st century and fourth best-selling album of all time, while its 23-week tenure atop the UK Albums Chart is the longest by a female solo artist. In the United States, the album held the top position for 24 weeks, longer than any other album since 1985 and the longest by a female solo artist in Billboard 200 history. It was certified Diamond by the RIAA and was ranked as the "Greatest Billboard 200 Album of All Time."

Five singles were released to promote the album, with "Rolling in the Deep," "Someone like You" and "Set Fire to the Rain" becoming international number-one songs, while "Rumour Has It" charted in the top 20 across Europe and North America. Globally, 21 was the biggest selling musical release for both 2011 and 2012, and helped revitalise lagging sales of the UK and US music industry. With 35 million copies sold worldwide, the album is one of the best-selling albums of all time. Critics hailed the album as a shift from the overtly sexual and musically bombastic status quo, and attributed its success to its deeply autobiographical yet universal songs.

Shortlisted for the 2011 Mercury Prize, 21 won the 2012 Grammy Award for Album of the Year and the Brit Award for British Album of the Year.

Writing and production

In April 2009, 20-year-old Adele, who had recently embarked on her first serious relationship with a man 10 years her senior, began composing the follow-up to her 2008 debut album 19. In response to the media's typecasting her as an "old soul" due to the vintage production and sentimental nature of her songs, Adele decided on a more upbeat and contemporary second album. However, studio sessions were generally unproductive and, after two weeks, yielded only one song recorded to the singer's satisfaction—the Jim Abbiss-produced "Take It All," a lovelorn piano ballad not unlike the songs on 19. Disillusioned with lack of inspiration and the slow progress of the studio sessions, she cancelled the remaining recording session dates.

Adele had written "Take It All" during a difficult moment in her relationship. When she played the song for her boyfriend, the two got into a bitter argument that culminated in the end of their 18-month relationship. Heartbroken but musically stimulated, Adele channelled her rush of emotions into her music, crafting songs that examined her failed relationship from the perspectives of vengeful ex-lover, heartbroken victim, and nostalgic old flame.

Writing for the album began shortly after Adele separated from her lover. Within a day of her break-up, she contacted producer Paul Epworth, intent on capturing her emotion in a song: "We'd had a fuming argument the night before ... I'd been bubbling. Then I went into the studio and screamed." Although she had initially planned on completing a ballad that she had begun writing with Epworth more than a year ago, the producer suggested that she aim for a more aggressive sound. Together, they restructured the song and re-wrote lyrics to reflect Adele's recent experience, deciding on the title "Rolling in the Deep." The instrumentation evolved organically—after trying out various jazz riffs, Adele attempted the first verse a cappella, inspiring Epworth to improvise a melody on his acoustic guitar. A thumping drum beat was set to mimic her racing heartbeat. In two days, a demo was recorded to be produced by Columbia Records co-president Rick Rubin later that year. However, Adele re-approached Epworth months later to complete production of the song.

British producer Fraser T Smith recalled following a similar trajectory when he teamed up with Adele to compose the subsequent third single "Set Fire to the Rain" at his MyAudiotonic Studios in London. After the two had created the demo, Adele revisited her co-writer to record the song with him, instead of the intended producer Rick Rubin. Smith thought Adele's first attempt superior to subsequent takes, and used the demo as the final production of the song, complete with live drum sounds and an elaborate strings section .

With the demos to two songs recorded, Adele approached American musician and OneRepublic frontman Ryan Tedder, who was in London at the time for a radio show. Tedder had expressed interest in collaborating with the singer after they met at the 2009 Grammy Awards ceremony in February. He arrived four hours early to their first studio session, buying time to better familiarise himself with some of her previous work. Although unaware of Adele's personal predicament, he composed the opening piano sequence and first few lines to what became the lovelorn ballad "Turning Tables": "Close enough to start a war/All that I have is on the floor." Coincidentally, it perfectly captured the experience of the singer, who arrived at the studio moments after another altercation with her former lover. Angry and unfocused, she denounced her ex-lover's tendency to "turn the tables" on her during their arguments, an expression that Tedder decided to reference in the song's lyrics. Adele recorded the demo with Jim Abbiss the following day.

Adele and Tedder arranged a second meeting and reconvened at Serenity West Studios in Los Angeles weeks later to write and record "Rumour Has It." In an interview, Tedder recalled his astonishment at the singer's musicality and vocal prowess after she completed the main vocals to the song in 10 minutes: "She sang it once top to bottom, pitch perfect, she didn't miss a note. I looked at the engineer then at her and said, 'Adele I don't know what to tell you but I have never had anyone do that in ten years'."

After working with Smith, Tedder, and Epworth, Adele travelled to the United States for the remainder of the album's production. At the suggestion of Columbia Records group president Ashley Newton, she met with songwriter Greg Wells at his studio in Culver City, Los Angeles, where they co-wrote the gospel-tinged ballad "One and Only." The song evolved from a four-chord piano progression in a 6/8-metre, which Wells had conceived before meeting with the singer. The lyrics, aimed at the singer's new love interest, came together quickly and were later completed with Dan Wilson, with whom she also composed "Someone Like You." In 2008, Adele's appearance on the NBC sketch comedy show Saturday Night Live caught the attention of producer Rick Rubin. In the initial stage of the album's production Rubin had signed on as its sole producer, and was scheduled to produce all of its songs. The demos she had recorded with Epworth, Smith, and Tedder were subsequently rerecorded by Rubin when she met with him in his Shangri-La Studio in Malibu, California in April 2010.

Rubin, notorious for his unorthodox production style, pushed the singer beyond her comfort zone, and despite being drawn to his unconventional methods, Adele described working with the producer as daunting. Rubin had attended many of her shows throughout 2008–2009, and after a Hollywood Bowl performance, approached her to compliment her live sound. When they met in Malibu, he attempted to "capture her live show across on record," assembling a team of musicians—including drummer Chris Dave, guitarist Matt Sweeney, James Poyser on piano, and Pino Palladino on bass—to contribute live instrumentation to the recording sessions. He also decided against the use of music samples and electronic instruments. An advocate of a more free-form approach to music-making, Rubin relied on the moods and feelings behind the music itself to guide the instrumental and melodic arrangement of the songs. He isolated the singer in the studio and encouraged her, as well as his team of musicians, to approach the production process with more spontaneity and less restraint. The singer even recalled moving the musicians and production team to tears while recording some of the songs. In an interview, he commented on the nature of the recording sessions:

After recording the album with Rubin, Adele was dissatisfied with many of the songs. Ultimately, she decided to scrap most work done in favour of the early takes she did with other producers, including Epworth and Tedder, in order for the music to reflect the raw emotion felt immediately after her break-up. From her collaboration with Rubin, only five songs appeared on the album: "Don't You Remember," "He Won't Go," "I'll Be Waiting," "One and Only," as well as the U.S-only track "I Found a Boy." Weeks after her stint with Rubin, Adele learned of her ex-lover's recent engagement, inspiring the composition of the album's final track "Someone Like You." Adele's record label was initially dissatisfied with the song's sparse production, which comprised Adele's voice alongside a sole piano, and requested that it be re-recorded with Rubin's band. However, the singer opted to keep the arrangement, stating that the song was personal to her and that she wrote it to "free herself."

Adele first intended to title the album Rolling in the Deep, her adaptation of the slang phrase "roll deep," which summarises how she felt about her relationship; in her loose translation, the phrase refers to having someone "that has your back" and always supports you. However, the singer later deemed the title too confusing for some of her audiences. Although she had wanted to avoid the number motif of her debut, Adele considered "21" the most fitting title as it represented her age at the time of the album's composition, serving as an autobiographical period piece, and symbolised the personal maturity and artistic evolution since her debut.

Music and influence

21 bears influences of Adele's extended exposure to the music of the Southern United States during the North American leg of her 2008–2009 tour An Evening with Adele. Frequent smoke breaks with her tour bus driver, a Nashville, Tennessee native, resulted in her introduction to bluegrass and rockabilly, and the music of Garth Brooks, Wanda Jackson, Alison Krauss, Lady Antebellum, Dolly Parton and Rascal Flatts. Adele developed an appreciation for the country genre, praising what she described as the immediacy of the themes and the straightforward narrative structure of many of the songs she listened to; she also expressed her enthusiasm at simply learning a new style of music. Although influenced by Adele's interest in country music at the time, 21 remains faithful to the Motown influences of 19 and exhibits both gospel and soul music inflections. Instruments such as the saxophone, harp, banjo and the accordion contributed to its exploration of blues and soul. The singer drew from the music of Mary J. Blige, Kanye West, Elbow, Mos Def, Alanis Morissette,

Tom Waits, and Sinéad O'Connor in the cultivation of the album's sound, and credited Yvonne Fair, Andrew Bird, Neko Case, and The Steel Drivers with its musical direction.

Adele's style on 21 is generally characterised by critics as soul, although some suggest that the album eschews any distinct stylistic epithet. John Murphy of musicOMH characterises the album as British soul. Jon Caramanica of The New York Times wrote that the album's music is a part of a recent British soul revival that "summoned styles dating back to Motown girl groups and Dusty Springfield." Ryan Reed of Paste calls Adele a "British alt-soul prodigy" and the album's music "the stuff of sensual modern pop-noir landscape, heavy on retro textures and relationship drama." Danyel Smith of Billboard views that Adele's music exhibits influences from Northern soul, Aretha Franklin, Sade, and Bette Midler.

Larry Flick of SiriusXM called 21 "a pop record with soul leanings," while The Washington Post's Allion Stewart commented on the album's eclectic nature: "Everything on is precisely calibrated to transcend genres, to withstand trends ... It's slightly angled toward country, even more toward R&B," and "informed, but never overwhelmed, by roots music." Mike Spies of Slate argues that soul music is inextricably linked to the political, historical, and cultural experience of African Americans, and that Adele and her contemporaries, far removed from this socio-cultural milieu, can offer only a mere duplicate of actual "soul," despite a capacity to convincingly channel the sound.

Songs

The sequence of the tracks on the deeply autobiographical album correlate to the range of emotions Adele experienced after the break-up, progressing from themes of anger and bitterness, to feelings of loneliness, heartbreak and regret, and finally acceptance. The revenge song "Rolling in the Deep," a "dark, bluesy, gospel, disco tune" in the singer's own words, was written as a "fuck you" to her ex-lover after his disparaging remarks that she was weak and that her life without him would be "boring and lonely and rubbish." Opening with an understated acoustic guitar strum, the song's first lines set the foreboding tone of the album. Pounding martial beats, shuffling percussion, and piano coalesce into a dramatic, multilayered chorus over which "Adele's voice ranges, dramatizing her search for just the right tone and words to express her dismay that a man would dare break her heart." The first single from 21, "Rolling in the Deep" is one of the more apparent influences of the bluesy Americana music that framed the album's sound.

"Rumour Has It," the singer's tongue-in-cheek retort to the hurtful gossip that surrounded her break-up, was aimed at her own friends for their part in spreading these rumours. Fusing elements of doo-wop and Tin Pan Alley blues, the percussion-driven song is built on girl-group harmonies, piano chords, pounding kick drum and handclaps, and finds the singer "channeling a '40s, piano-vixen lounge singer." Jon Caramanica of The New York Times pointed out the song's "hollow counterpoint vocals" and slow, "daringly morbid" bridge that veers from the pounding rhythm before once again acceding to it. In the studio, Tedder experimented with a riff inspired by Radiohead's "I Might Be Wrong," crediting the song's drop D tuning and American blues vibe as impetus for "Rumour Has It." In "Turning Tables," a song of domestic dispute, its narrator assumes a defensive stance against a manipulative ex-lover. Reconciling herself with the termination of a contentious relationship, she vows emotional distance to shield herself from future heartbreak. Bryan Boyd of The Irish Times likened the singer to 1980s Welsh rocker Bonnie Tyler in delivering the vocals with a mixture of anger, pain and pathos. According to Paste magazine, cinematic strings "serve as fitting counterpoint to heartbroken, hollowed-out lyrics."

The Rick Rubin-produced fourth track "Don't You Remember," co-written by Adele and Dan Wilson, marks a shift in the album's theme, from anger and defensiveness to reflection and heartbreak. A downtempo country music-styled ballad, the song was added late to the production of the album after the singer grew ashamed of her continued negative portrayal of her ex-lover throughout the album. Its lyrics entreat a past lover to remember the happier moments at the beginning of a now broken relationship. In "Set Fire to the Rain" the singer delineates the conflicting stages of a troubled union and wrestles with her inability to fully let go. Accentuated by ornate orchestral flourishes, swirling strings, crescendos, and dramatic vocal effects towards its climactic end, the song stands in stark contrast to the otherwise understated production of the album, and in reviews, was characterised by critics as a pop rock power ballad. To achieve a fuller sound, producer Fraser T Smith incorporated the popular "wall of sound" reverberative technique in framing the song's dense instrumentation.

"Take It All," the seventh track, written and recorded with Francis "Eg" White and Jim Abbis before the breakdown of Adele's relationship, is a piano and vocal ballad that borrows heavily from pop, soul and gospel. In his review of 21, Allmusic's Matt Collar called the song the album's centrepiece, "an instant-classic" in the same vein as "And I Am Telling You I'm Not Going," and "All by Myself," and a "cathartic moment for fans who identify with their idol's Pyrrhic lovelorn persona." The track precedes "I'll

Be Waiting," the second of two songs produced by Epworth, which diverges from the scathing "Rolling in the Deep" in its optimistic tone and brisk, lilted melody. A protagonist's mea culpa for a relationship gone wrong, she declares to wait patiently for her lover's inevitable return. The song was compared to the work of Aretha Franklin for its "huge vocal sound on the chorus, rolling piano and boxy snare," while Tom Townshend of MSN Music described its brass section as a Rolling Stones-esque "barroom gospel."

Although the album predominantly explores the singer's failed relationship, not all songs were geared towards her ex-lover. "He Won't Go," a nod to hip hop and contemporary R&B, was a tribute to a friend who battled heroin addiction. The ninth track "One and Only," noted for its gospel-tinged vocals, organ, and choir, was directed at a close friend for whom Adele shared romantic feelings. And "Lovesong" was dedicated to Adele's mother and friends, in whom she found solace when she grew homesick and lonely while recording in Malibu.

The album closes with the "heartbreak adagio" "Someone Like You," a soft piano ballad that pairs Adele's vocals with a looping piano melody. In interviews, the singer described it as the summation of her attitude towards her ex-lover by the end of the album's production. The song's lyrics describe a protagonist's attempt at dealing with her heartbreak after she learns of her ex-lover's recent marriage and happy new life. Sean Fennessey of The Village Voice praised the singer's nuanced vocal performance in the song, which ascends "into a near-shrieked whisper" during parts of the chorus, after which she once again regains composure. One of the more commended songs on the album, "Someone Like You" was praised for its lyrical depth and understated simplicity.

Release and promotion

For the North American release of 21 on 22 February, Columbia Records executives used the "'long tail' sales theory" to shape its marketing campaign, which, according to Columbia senior VP of marketing Scott Greer, entailed "building a critical mass throughout February in order to reach all those people who bought 19." Key to this was the record company approaching internet and media partners Vevo, AOL and VH1 to begin promoting Adele's old and new songs. In the months leading up to the European release of 21, Adele embarked on a promotional tour across Europe, performing on the UK's Royal Variety Performance on 9 December 2010, the finale of reality singing competition The Voice of Holland on 21

January 2011, and on BBC Radio 1's Live Lounge on six days later. On 24 January 2011, during the week of the album's UK release, she performed an acoustic set of selected songs from 21 at London's Tabernacle music hall, which was screened live on her personal website. Adele performed "Someone Like You" at the 2011 BRIT Awards ceremony, which was well received and resulted in a sales increase for both 19 and 21.

From September to October 2010, Adele embarked on a mini-promotional tour of the US, which included stops in New York and Minneapolis, as well as an exclusive appearance at the famous Club Largo in Los Angeles. Although she did not use Twitter at the time, Columbia created an account that redirected followers to the singer's personal blog. Throughout February, Adele's personal site hosted a "21 Days of Adele" promotion, which featured exclusive daily content, including a live chat and a video of the singer explaining the inspiration for each album track. The week of release was also accompanied by a spate of television appearances on many American daytime and late-night talk shows, such as the Today Show on 18 February, Late Show with David Letterman on 21 February, and The Ellen DeGeneres Show and Jimmy Kimmel Live! on 24 February. Adele performed "Someone Like You" at the 2011 MTV Video Music Awards ceremony.

Adele embarked on her second concert tour Adele: Live in support of 21, scheduling more than 60 shows across Europe and North America. The shows received positive reviews, many of which noted the show's understated nature, the singer's vocal performance and her accessible persona. However, recurring health and vocal problems led to numerous alterations to the tour itinerary. The cancellation of the North American leg of the tour was due to a vocal haemorrhage on her vocal cords. The singer underwent corrective vocal surgery in November 2011 and cancelled all public appearances until February 2012. Adele performed "Rolling in the Deep" at the 2011 ECHO Awards, 2012 Grammy Awards and 2012 BRIT Awards ceremonies.

21 yielded five singles in total, including four worldwide releases. The lead single "Rolling in the Deep" was released in November 2010, and peaked the charts in the Netherlands, Germany, Belgium, Italy, and Switzerland. It became a top-ten hit in Austria, Canada, Denmark, Ireland, New Zealand, and Norway. Released in the UK on 16 January 2011, it peaked at number two. In the US, the song became "the most widely crossed over song of the past twenty-five years," appearing on a record 12 different Billboard charts . The song spent seven consecutive weeks at the top of the Hot 100, and was ranked the top song and the best-selling song of the year.

"Someone like You" debuted at number 36 on the UK Singles Chart due to strong digital sales, and after falling to number 47, it ascended to number one when the singer performed it at the 2011 BRIT Awards. It peaked at number one in Australia, New Zealand, Italy, Finland, France, Switzerland, and the US. "Set Fire to the Rain," the third single, topped the singles chart in the US, the Netherlands and Belgium , and reached the top five in Switzerland, Italy and Austria. "Rumour Has It" was confirmed as the fourth and final official US single from the album by Ryan Tedder at the Grammy Awards in 2012, and was released 1 March 2012. In some countries, "Turning Tables" was released as the fourth single. It was the fifth single to be released to US mainstream stations, although it received limited airplay due to an unofficial release. Even though "I'll Be Waiting" was never released as a single, it charted at No. 29 on the US Triple A chart.

Critical reception

21 received generally positive reviews from critics. At Metacritic, which assigns a normalised rating out of 100 to reviews from mainstream publications, the album received an average score of 76, based on 34 reviews. In the Chicago Tribune, Greg Kot deemed the music an improvement over 19, writing that "21 beefs up the rhythmic drive and the

drama of the arrangements." Simon Harper of Clash wrote, " two years ... she's clearly seen the world. Where 19 marked the turbulent swan song to a teenage life, 21 introduces the realities of adult life, where grown-up responsibilities collide with heartache and emotional scars run deep." John Murphy of MusicOMH said that it shared the themes of "pain, sadness and anger" explored on Amy Winehouse's Back to Black , while hailing 21 as "one of the great 'break-up' albums, and the first truly impressive record of 2011." Sputnikmusic's Joseph Viney stated that 21 combined the "best bits of Aretha Franklin's old-school soul with Lauryn Hill's sass and sense of cynical modern femininity." Sean Fennessey from The Village Voice wrote that the album "has a diva's stride and a diva's purpose. With a touch of sass and lots of grandeur, it's an often magical thing that insists on its importance ... the line here between melodrama and pathos is wafer-thin, and Adele toes it deftly. It's what separates her from her contemporaries in the mid-'00s wave of British white-girl r&b-dom." Q commented that, despite a "slightly scattershot quality ... greatness is tantalizingly within reach." In The New York Times, Jon Pareles applauded the singer's emotive timbre, comparing her to Dusty Springfield, Petula Clark, and Annie Lennox: " can seethe, sob, rasp, swoop, lilt and belt, in ways that draw more attention to the song than to the singer." Ryan Reed of Paste regarded her voice as "a raspy, aged-beyond-its-years thing of full-blooded beauty," while MSN Music's Tom Townshend declared her "the finest singer of generation."

Matthew Cole from Slant Magazine was less impressed, believing Adele's vocals masked the "blandness" of many of the songs, a fault that he said would have been more apparent had they been performed by a lesser talent. Allison Stewart of The Washington Post claimed that many tracks were remarkable "only because Adele is singing them." Robert Christgau gave the album a two-star honourable mention in his consumer guide for MSN Music, writing that "part of me likes how many albums this proud white-soul normal has sold, but the part that likes fast ones wins."

Commercial performance

21 debuted at number one on the UK Albums Chart on 30 January 2011 with first-week sales of 208,000 copies. While in its fourth consecutive week at number one, Adele performed "Someone Like You" at the 2011 BRIT Awards, resulting in a sales surge of 890 percent on Amazon.co.uk within an hour of the show's broadcast. 19 climbed to number four on the UK Albums Chart, while on the singles chart, "Someone like You" leaped from 47 to number one, and "Rolling in the Deep" climbed from five to four. Adele became the first living act since The Beatles in 1964 to have two UK top

five albums and singles simultaneously. A week later, 19 rose to number 2 in its 102nd week of release, this made Adele the first act to occupy the chart's top two spots since The Corrs in 1999. 21 achieved separate consecutive number-one spells during its 2011 chart run on the UK Albums Chart, claiming the top spot for 11 straight weeks between February and April 2011, then for five consecutive weeks between April and June, and then for another two weeks in July 2011. In January 2012, a year after its release, the album reclaimed the top spot of the charts, and on 15 April 2012 it returned once again to the top. It amassed 23 weeks at number one to date. Midway through 2012, 21 was the best-selling album of the year despite being released in early 2011. In December 2012, 21 overtook Oasis' Morning Glory? to become the fourth best-selling album of all time in the UK. By December 2012, 21 had spent 101 weeks in the UK Albums Chart Top 75, including 95 weeks in the Top 40, 76 weeks in the Top 10 and 23 weeks at number one. It has sold a total of 4,944,516 copies as of July 2016, making the biggest selling album since 2000 in the UK. and fourth biggest seller of all time there.

Globally, 21 is the best-selling album of the past decade according to the International Federation of the Phonographic Industry, and topped the charts in more than 30 countries. In July 2012, the album was certified decuple platinum by the International Federation of the Phonographic Industry, denoting sales of ten million copies across Europe, making it the highest-certified album in Europe since the IFPI Platinum Europe award was launched in 1996. The album spent 38 nonconsecutive weeks at the top of the Belgian Albums Chart . It led the Switzerland Schweizer Hitparade Top 100 Albums chart for 14 weeks, and the French Chart for 18 weeks. In the Netherlands, 21 debuted at number one on 29 January 2011, and topped the chart for 30 weeks. It has remained in the top 10 as of February 2012. In Germany, it led the chart for eight weeks. The album lodged 35 weeks atop the Irish Albums Chart, the longest in the chart's history, and sold over 270,000 copies. Charting 124 weeks in Finland from early 2011 to summer of 2013 and re-entering in early 2014, 21 became the second-longest-charting album of all time in the country behind Keskiviikko... 40 ensimmäistä hittiä by Leevi and the Leavings. It became the fifth-best selling album of 2011 and 2012 in Finland, with quadruple-platinum sales to date .

21 spent 32 weeks at number-one on the Australian ARIA Top 50 Albums Chart, 10 of which were consecutive. Adele also replicated her UK chart record when she achieved two titles in the top five of the ARIA Album and Singles chart simultaneously: in the week ending 17 July 2011, "Someone

Like You" and "Rolling in the Deep" occupied positions one and four respectively on the Singles Chart, while 21 and 19 held at number one and three on the Albums Charts. In December 2012, it was announced that 21 was nearing sales of one million in Australia. This makes 21 only the seventh album to ever achieve this fete in Australia and the first to do so since Delta Goodrem's Innocent Eyes. On the New Zealand RIANZ Albums Chart, 21 debuted at number-one in January 2011, and spent 28 weeks at the summit in 2011. It reclaimed the top of the chart in January 2012, and spent the anniversary of its release at number one. Except for a single week at number six on the week ending 21 November 2011, the album remained in the top five for 70 consecutive weeks. Its 38 accumulated weeks at the top is the longest in New Zealand chart history.

Released 22 February in the US, 21 debuted at number one on the Billboard 200 with first-week sales of 352,000 copies. The album remained in the top three for its first 24 weeks, the top five for a record 39 consecutive weeks, and the top 10 for a total of 84 weeks, That staggering sum ties the album with Bruce Springsteen's Born in the U.S.A. for the second-most weeks in the region. 21 became the best-selling digital album of all time in the US, selling 6 million copies by January 2012. On 17 May 2012, 21 became the 29th album since 1991 to sell over 9 million copies in the United States and became the first album in the United States to sell that amount since Usher's Confessions reached sales of 9 million in 2005. By November 2012, it has sold 10 million copies, a feat achieved in 92 weeks, making it the fastest album to sell 10 million since 'N Sync's No Strings Attached in 2001. In February 2015, it was announced that the album had spent 208 straight weeks, or four years, on the Billboard 200 chart, spending only 24 of those weeks outside the Top 100. As of February 2016, 21 has sold 11.7 million copies in the United States, becoming the tenth largest-selling album since Nielsen Music started tracking sales in 1991. The album's performance on the Billboard 200 chart earned 21 the distinction of all-time number one album on the chart, according to a summary performed by Billboard in November 2015. In Canada, 21 spent 28 weeks at number one, and was certified diamond in January 2012 by Music Canada for shipment of 800,000 copies of the album. 21 had sold over 1.489 million copies by January 2013, making it the third best-selling album in Canada, since Nielsen SoundScan started tracking sales.

Accolades

The album was nominated for the 2011 Barclaycard Mercury Prize. In November 2011, Adele won three American Music Awards including

Favorite Pop/Rock Album for 21. Adele has seven Grammys for 21, in February 2012 she won the Grammy Awards for Album of the Year and Best Pop Vocal Album for 21, Record of the Year, Song of the Year and Best Short Form Music Video for "Rolling in the Deep," and Best Pop Solo Performance for "Someone Like You." Her producer, Paul Epworth won Producer of the Year, Non-Classical. In February 2013, a live rendition of the album's third single "Set Fire to the Rain," included on Live at the Royal Albert Hall, won the Grammy Award for Best Pop Solo Performance. On 21 February 2012, 21 won the British MasterCard Album of the Year at the 2012 BRIT Awards. It also won the 2012 Juno Award for International Album of the Year.

21 appeared on many year-end best-of lists. The album was ranked the best album of the year by the Associated Press, The Austin Chronicle, Entertainment Weekly, Star Tribune, Digital Spy, MSN Music, New York Daily News, Rolling Stone, TIME magazine, and editors of USA Today. Critics at Billboard voted the album number-one of the year, while Scottish newspaper the Daily Record, editors of Amazon and the editors at Rhapsody also ranked the album at number one. The album appeared in the runner-up spot on MTV's list of the Best Albums of 2011 as well as lists produced by The Boston Globe, The Hollywood Reporter and Toronto Sun. It placed

within the top 10 on lists produced by American Songwriter, Q, Los Angeles Times, Clash, and The Washington Post. "Rolling in the Deep" consistently placed high on various year-end critics' list, and was ranked the best song of the year in The Village Voice's Pazz and Jop mass critics' poll. In 2012, Rolling Stone ranked the album number six on its list of Women Who Rock: The 50 Greatest Albums of All Time. As of January 2015, Billboard named 21 as the third best album of the 2010s .

Legacy

In September 2011, Adele claimed Guinness World Records for becoming the first female artist to have two singles and two albums in the UK top five simultaneously. 21 also became the first album in UK chart history to reach sales of three million copies in a calendar year, and set records for the most consecutive weeks with a UK number-one album with 11 weeks , and the most cumulative weeks at number one in the UK. It sold 4 million copies by February 2012 and by March, it had been certified 16-times platinum by the British Phonographic Industry for shipments of 4,500,000 units, the highest ever certified album in the UK. It is also the most downloaded album in UK history, the biggest-selling album of the 21st century in the UK, and the 4th best selling album in the UK of all time. Sales of 21 helped increase XL

Recordings', Adele's record label, bank balance from £3million to £32million in the space of 12 months. In late November 2012, 21 fell out of the Top 40 of the UK Albums Chart for the first time since its release in January 2011.

With 21, Adele became the first female to have three singles simultaneously in the top 10 of the Billboard Hot 100 as a solo artist. In the week ending 23 February 2012, she also became the first female artist to place two titles in the top five of both the Billboard 200 and Hot 100 concurrently, with 21 and 19 occupying number one and number four on the Billboard 200 respectively, and "Set Fire to the Rain" and "Rolling in the Deep" at number two and five respectively. On 14 June 2012, 21 scored its 24th week atop the US album charts, the longest since Prince's Purple Rain finished a non-consecutive 24-week run in 1985. The album is also the longest-running number-one by a UK studio album , the longest-running number-one album by a female solo artist ever in the US, and the longest-running number-one in the SoundScan era. The album also spent 24 non-consecutive weeks at number 2.

21 is credited with saving the first quarter album sales of 2012 in the United States. Without 21, the first quarter of 2012 would have been down 3.4%

compared to the first quarter of 2011. 21 sold more copies in the first quarter of 2012 than any album since 2005 and is the oldest album to be the best-selling album in the first quarter of the year since No Doubt's Tragic Kingdom in 1997. On 28 November 2012, the Recording Industry Association of America certified it Diamond after having sold more than 10 million copies in the United States alone; it is the first album released in the 2010s to achieve Diamond certification. In December 2012, it was announced that 21 was the best-selling album on iTunes for two years in a row.

21 was the best-selling album of both 2011 and 2012 in the United States and Canada despite being over a year old. It is the first album to be the best-selling album two years in a row since Michael Jackson's Thriller was the best-selling album of 1983 and 1984. Despite being over a year old, 21 sold more copies in 2012 than the best-selling albums of 2006 through 2010 sold in their respective years. It is also one of only four albums in the Nielsen SoundScan era to sell over 4 million copies in each of two calendar years. Due to these successes, Billboard declared Adele the Artist of the Year for the second year in a row, making her the first artist to receive the honour twice. In February 2013, it was announced that 21 had spent two full years on the Billboard 200, never charting lower than number 35 on the chart. This

makes 21 the best-selling album of the past 10 years and the fifth best-selling album released since January 2000. In March 2013, after Adele won an Academy Award for "Skyfall," the album reentered the Top 10 of the Billboard 200. This marked the album's 81st week in the Top 10. Only two other albums have spent as much time in the Top 10: Born in the U.S.A. and The Sound of Music. In November 2013, it was announced that 21 had become the first album to sell three million digital copies in the United States and that the album is the 13th best-selling overall in the United States since Nielsen SoundScan began tracking sales in 1991.

Impact and response

The album's success has been attributed to its cross-cultural appeal, which has catered to fans of various genres of pop, adult contemporary and R&B, as well as various generations and musical timelines. According to Sasha Frere-Jones of The New Yorker the album's success in the US can be attributed to its target audience—that is, "middle-aged moms ... the demographic that decides American elections." Critics also suggest that the album's understated musical production and relative lack of artifice are striking deviations from the "bombastic theatrics" of the mainstream music industry. Ethan Smith of The Wall Street Journal found that Adele's "deliberately unflashy" nature, full figure, and "everywoman" appeal gave her a lucrative niche in the market, while her tendency to emphasise "substance over style" made her the "Anti-Lady Gaga." Guy Adams of The Independent argued that 21's success signals the re-emergence of the more traditional approach to commercial success:

With the release of 21, critics began to tout Adele as the new torchbearer for the British soul music that ascended to the American mainstream via Duffy, Joss Stone, Amy Winehouse and Lily Allen. Although the initial popularity of these artists in the early 2000s incited the media to declare a "new wave of British invasion," Joseph Viney of Sputnikmusic saw their subsequent absence as an opportunity for Adele to "stake her claim as the UK's leading solo female artist." John Murphy of MusicOMH declared the album "a timely reminder that British soul hasn't lost its mojo." Indie label XL Recordings founder Richard Russell discussed what be believed to be the quasi-subversiveness of 21's chart dominance. Characterising the success of 21 as "almost political and sort of radical," Russell stated that the lack of gimmicks in Adele's music undermined the widespread perception that female performers have to conform to specific body-types, or imbue their music with gratuitous sexual imagery, in order attain success.

Printed in Great Britain
by Amazon

71087732R00037